Suffolk Steam Railways

David Kindred

Old Pond
PUBLISHING LTD

SUFFOLK STEAM RAILWAYS

First published 2009

ISBN 978-1-906853-17-4

A catalogue record for this book is available from the British Library

Published by
Old Pond Publishing Ltd
Dencora Business Centre
36 White House Road
Ipswich
IP1 5LT
United Kingdom

www.oldpond.com

Title page photograph: J15 65467 on the 'Weedkiller' train near Marlesford
on the Framlingham branch line.

Frontispiece: Britannia Class 70005 *John Milton* entering the Ipswich tunnel
from the Stoke side, 6 June 1959. The Ipswich Locoshed with
its coaling tower and the Cliff Quay power station are in the
background. (Photo by Aubrey Frost.)

Cover and book design by Liz Whatling
Printed in Malta by Gutenberg Press

Contents

Introduction

For over a hundred years, from the middle of the 19th century to the middle of the 20th century the nation relied mainly on steam power for the railways to carry people and freight. Steam held a fascination for many because everyone could see its power, the way pistons moved in and out of the cylinders, the movement of the connecting and coupling rods, the steam and smoke and, perhaps above all else, the noise of an engine working.

1968 saw the end of regular steam operation on British Railways but there remains a deep interest, kept alive by the many preserved railways and steam locomotives that run on them and on the main lines.

This book looks at the part that steam locomotives played in Suffolk. We were not over-endowed with railway lines. Many that were built in this predominantly agricultural county were soon losing money and eventually closed.

Steam locomotives consist of very heavy pieces of metal that require accurate machining and fitting. The fire needs lighting up hours before they can be used. Ipswich Locoshed was extremely primitive, with most work carried on outside in the elements. There was no Health and Safety regime, either.

The railways were a major employer in East Anglia, with Ipswich Locoshed having 450 employees on the books to run over ninety locomotives. To that figure must be added the permanent way staff who maintained the track, the signal and telegraph section, the goods yard staff, the station staff and so on. Even small stations could provide jobs for a couple of dozen people.

Drivers earned their place in the hierarchy by their experience built up by years of firstly cleaning, before firing and then driving; initially on small shunting locomotives, then goods trains, before passenger trains and, finally, crack express trains. There were few 'fail safe' devices. The safety of the trains depended on train crews seeing and interpreting the signals by the trackside and the driver controlling the speed around curves and crossings. Timekeeping was of paramount importance and the firemen had to shovel tons of coal so that the drivers could maintain schedules.

The railways were a seven days a week, 24-hour, round-the-clock business that demanded shift work, irregular hours and for some, regularly lodging away from home. Against this background of hard work and unsocial hours grew a strong sense of camaraderie and fierce loyalty to their depot and line. Richard 'Dick' Hardy was most impressed with the Ipswich men when he was responsible for Ipswich Locoshed in the early 1950s.

David Kindred has been collecting photographs for many years. He is a professional photographer, not a railway enthusiast. In selecting photographs for this book, he realised that he lacked the technical knowledge to caption the photographs. John Day, a local railway enthusiast and Chairman of the Ipswich Transport Society, readily agreed to help with the captions and enlisted the help of several other local enthusiasts, including Graham Hardinge, John Yelverton and David Chappell.

While a lot of the photographs stir the emotions with steam engines storming across the countryside or meandering along the idyllic scenery of some branch line, let us not forget the photographers, without whom this book would not be possible. The photographs were taken when a camera was not a small pocket-sized implement but a large device to be carried, often across fields or along tracks, to some favourite spot that provided a good location for the photograph. There was much skill in selecting the right lens, the right aperture, the right shutter speed

and even the right film to get that image of a steam engine speeding along.

Thanks to David Kindred for creating this selection for you to enjoy and also the likes of the Titshall Brothers, Aubrey Frost, Dr Ian C Allen, H N 'Jimmy' James and those other photographers who took the trouble to record an era now long gone.

Brian Dyes
Archives Manager, Ipswich Transport Museum

Preface

I know little about railway locomotives and the days of steam.

This may seem an odd thing for me to say – but my expertise is in photography. For about twenty years I have been accumulating and archiving vintage photographs of Suffolk which have come to me in all forms including single prints and boxes of glass negatives. These days computer technology means that I have been able to restore many damaged and faded images. The pictures from broken glass-plate negatives can be rebuilt to look like new.

While I could have written brief captions to most of the photographs in this book

I needed to ask railway experts for the real details. I have collated negative files, newspapers cuttings, notes attached to prints and technical information from those credited in the Acknowledgements on page 127.

Where possible I have named the photographers who did such a brilliant job of capturing stream power on our railways. They recorded not just the locomotives thundering across the county but also the station staff and sometimes tragic accidents.

My particular thanks go to Brian Dyes, Archives Manager, Ipswich Transport Museum for his help and Introduction to the book.

David Kindred
Ipswich, 2009

J15 65447 departing Stowmarket station with the last 'School train' from Stowmarket heading for the Mid Suffolk Light Railway line July 25 1952. The service took pupils from the Stowmarket Secondary and Grammar Schools to Haughley then along the line, departing daily at 4.25 pm

Main Lines, Stations and Services

1. Ipswich station, seen from Stoke Hill in 1860, was opened on 1 July that year. In the background is the River Orwell. Russell House on the right was close to where Constantine Road is now. The original Ipswich station was off Station Street, work on the line from Colchester having started in June 1846.

SUFFOLK STEAM RAILWAYS

2. Ipswich station as it was before the island platform was built in 1883. Stoke Hill is in the background. The windmill on top of the hill was taken down in 1887. (Photo by William Vick.)

3. Ipswich station in the late 1890s with the then new island platform built to deal with the increase of traffic. (Photo by William Vick.)

MAIN LINES, STATIONS AND SERVICES

4. Ipswich station from the junction with Princes Street in around 1915. The open-topped Great Eastern Railway Company bus ran a service to Shotley. Waterproof sheets were available for passengers during wet weather. The bus was one of twelve built in 1905 in the railway company's Stratford works, costing around £600 each. The service to Shotley started in 1905 and ran until 1916. The service re-started in 1919 and was later sold to the Eastern Counties Road Car Company Ltd.

5. Tavern Street, Ipswich in 1897. On the left, at the junction with Tower Street, the Great Eastern Railway Company had a booking office.

SUFFOLK STEAM RAILWAYS

6. & 7.   Passengers boarding a third class compartment at Ipswich station in 1909. Third class came to an end in 1956 when it was renamed 'Second'. British Rail later renamed this Standard class.

MAIN LINES, STATIONS AND SERVICES

8. The platforms at Ipswich were lit by gas lamps when this photograph was taken in around 1930.

9. Ipswich station in around 1910. In the centre road a horse is shunting a box wagon. The photographer was near the bridge over Ancaster Road.

SUFFOLK STEAM RAILWAYS

Cromer Express Disaster, 12.7.13.

CROMER EXPRESS DISASTER, No.10.

10. & 11.   Two trains collided at Colchester North station on Saturday 12 July 1913 when the London to
Cromer Express was diverted onto the wrong track, smashing into the back of a slow-moving
goods train. The crew of the express were two men from Ipswich. Driver William Barnard and
fireman Sidney Keeble were both killed along with the guard on the goods train.

MAIN LINES, STATIONS AND SERVICES

12. William Barnard's coffin being carried from his home in Rectory Road, Ipswich to the waiting horse-drawn hearse.

13. The funeral of Sidney Keeble, who was a member of the Ipswich Ambulance Corps, set off from his Wherstead Road home for Bramford church. Hundreds of people lined the streets for the funerals of both men.

SUFFOLK STEAM RAILWAYS

14. Crowds lined the tracks at Ipswich station on 30 April and 1 May 1932 to see a unique locomotive which had been prepared in secrecy. LNER locomotive 10000 had a radical design including a super heater and an extremely high-pressure boiler. It gained the nick-name 'Hush Hush'. It was a one-off design by Sir Nigel Gresley, the creator of the *Flying Scotsman* and later the *Mallard*.

MAIN LINES, STATIONS AND SERVICES

15. A Sandringham class B17, 61666 *Nottingham Forest* at Ipswich. The smoke box reporting number suggests this was probably a summer Saturday holiday extra from East Anglia's coastal resorts.

16. B17/4 61669 *Barnsley* leaving Ipswich with an express passenger train in the 1950s.

SUFFOLK STEAM RAILWAYS

17. Staff at Ipswich station in 1895.

18. Four locos hooked up at Ipswich station as they head for the Croft Street loco shed. This photograph is thought to be from 22 June 1935 when Sandringham class B17 2845 (second in line) was named *The Suffolk Regiment* at Ipswich to celebrate the regiment's 250th anniversary.

MAIN LINES, STATIONS AND SERVICES

19. B12 61570 at the south end of Ipswich station.

20. Long-serving Ipswich railwaymen Gordon Barber (right) and driver Fred Gibbs on B12 61570 at the end of platform three at Ipswich station in the 1950s.

MAIN LINES, STATIONS AND SERVICES

21. Ipswich station from near the entrance to the tunnel on the main Ipswich to London line in the 1950s. The sidings off to the right have now gone. The Station Hotel, at the junction of Princes Street, is on the extreme right. The position of the crew would suggest that the B1 is about to come off the train and be replaced by the Britannia on the right in the loco sidings.

SUFFOLK STEAM RAILWAYS

22. B17 61618 *Wynyard Park* with coaching stock out of the 'Foundout' (carriage sidings) at Ipswich station around 1957. This locomotive was withdrawn at Doncaster in 1960.

23. LNER J15 reclassified from GER Y14, number 7538 coming out of the Ipswich tunnel in 1937 probably with freight from Griffin Wharf. This locomotive was built in October 1888 and was withdrawn in December 1938.

MAIN LINES, STATIONS AND SERVICES

24. B12 8540 at the end of platform two at Ipswich station with an 'up' train.

25. Sandringham 61625 *Raby Castle* passes through Ipswich's centre road non-stop with probably a 'Summer Saturday Holiday Extra' from the East Suffolk line. Similar 61631 *Serlby Hall* waits at platform two. (Photo by H N James.)

SUFFOLK STEAM RAILWAYS

26. Elephants of Chipperfield's Circus parade along Ranelagh Road, Ipswich after arriving in the town by rail in March 1955. In the background is the Ancaster Road bridge and Ipswich station.

27. A large crowd gathered at Ipswich station to watch as the Household Cavalry headed along Princes Street after arriving in the town by train in the 1950s. This photograph was taken from the Station Hotel with Ranelagh Road in the background.

MAIN LINES, STATIONS AND SERVICES

28. Circus animals being loaded onto a lorry after arriving at Ipswich by train.

29. Elephants from a visiting circus leaving Ipswich station in the 1950s after arriving in town by train. The animals were paraded through town to promote the visit. Circuses used a site at the junction of London Road and Ranelagh Road or Christchurch Park during their stay. The houses in Ranelagh Road (right background) were demolished around 1960.

MAIN LINES, STATIONS AND SERVICES

30. Ipswich station in 1951 as locomotive 70000 Britannia arrived with the inaugral Norfolkman express train from London to Norwich.

31. Claud Hamilton D16 number 8880 pilots a Sandringham class locomotive out of Ipswich in around 1930.

32. B12 8505 coming out of the Ipswich tunnel heading for platform four. On the left are the sidings signal for locomotives coming out of the tunnel into the loco sidings behind the London end of platform two (see Plates 21 and 34).

MAIN LINES, STATIONS AND SERVICES

33. Ipswich Station from the Princes Street bridge in around 1905. This view features a pair of electric trams, which were in service from 1903 to 1926. They linked the station with the Cornhill. The electric trams replaced a horse-drawn service which operated this route from October 1880.

34. On 25 March 1965 the Departmental Steam Heating B1 number 17 is at the tunnel end of Ipswich station with the signal off for the locomotive to go through the tunnel to Croft Street Locoshed. It has spent the night heating carriages in the carriage sidings. (Photo by H N James.)

35. B12 8507 in excellent condition at Ipswich station in the 1930s.

36. Britannia 70012 *John of Gaunt* comes out of the Ipswich tunnel with a Liverpool Street to Norwich Express.

MAIN LINES, STATIONS AND SERVICES

37. E4 Class 2-4-0 at platform four of Ipswich station with a stopping train, probably for Bury St Edmunds.

38. 62543 leaving Ipswich probably for Cambridge. Immediately behind the engine is a North Eastern Region Clerestory coach. This photograph was taken from Gippeswyk Park. (Photo by H N James.)

SUFFOLK STEAM RAILWAYS

39. Class B12 61570 heading out of Ipswich near Bostock Road.

40. 61618 *Wynyard Park* with the 2.45 Ipswich to Liverpool Street at Belstead Bank 10 April 1952.
   (Photo by H N James.)

MAIN LINES, STATIONS AND SERVICES

41. B1 61052 near Ipswich on the 'Easterling' train between London, Lowestoft and Yarmouth. It was the only passenger train to run non-stop through Ipswich station. A note by Ipswich shed master Richard Hardy names the crew as 'Sanders and Cape'.

42. B1 61059 pulling one of the line's prestige express trains at Belstead Bank. (Photo by H N James.)

SUFFOLK STEAM RAILWAYS

43. An Ipswich to Yarmouth train leaving Ipswich. Shed master Richard Hardy noted that the crew on this run were 'Skeat and Broad'.

44. 61620 *Clumber* approaching Ipswich station under the impressive signal gantry with the Glasgow to Colchester through train. (Photo by H N James.)

MAIN LINES, STATIONS AND SERVICES

45. K3 61959 2-6-0 heading an up train past Bentley in the 1950s. These engines were mainly used for freight but on some occasions for passenger trains. (Photo by Aubrey Frost.)

46. B1 61056 heading south at Bentley in the 1950s. (Photo by Aubrey Frost.)

MAIN LINES, STATIONS AND SERVICES

47. Britannia Pacific 70037 *Hereward the Wake* climbs through Bentley with a Liverpool Street to Norwich Express. (Photo by Aubrey Frost.)

SUFFOLK STEAM RAILWAYS

48. Britannia class 70008 *Black Prince* heads a Norwich to Liverpool Street train past Bentley.
(Photo by Aubrey Frost.)

49. Britannia Pacific class 70035 *Rudyard Kipling* at Bentley in the 1950s. (Photo by Aubrey Frost.)

MAIN LINES, STATIONS AND SERVICES

50. B1 61055 heading for London with a milk train in 1950. There are road tankers on the three six-
wheeled wagons behind the locomotive. Most milk trains originated at Halesworth. (Photo by Aubrey Frost.)

51. B1 class locomotive 61252 at Bentley.

52. B1 61270 working hard with an up train at Bentley. This photograph is 1956 or after as the British Rail emblem on the tender was introduced that year. (Photo by Aubrey Frost.)

53. The last of the Sandringham class 61672 *West Ham United* at Bentley after 1956. (Photo by Aubrey Frost.)

MAIN LINES, STATIONS AND SERVICES

54. K1 62068 heads an up train at Bentley in the 1950s. (Photo by Aubrey Frost.)

55. B1 61378 storming through Bentley in March 1959. (Photo by Aubrey Frost.)

MAIN LINES, STATIONS AND SERVICES

56. B17 class locomotive 2814, later renumbered 61614 in the LNER numbering scheme and named *Hedingham Castle,* heading a train through Brantham under what is now the A137 high-arch bridge.

57. A tender-first J39 0-6-0 number 64724 brings a train into Ipswich yard while a sister engine shunts the Hadleigh Road end of the yard. A 1950s photograph taken from the London Road bridge.

58. B1 61201 crossing the River Gipping near Sproughton. The train has just left the East Suffolk junction and is heading towards Stowmarket. In the distance is the bridge carrying the East Suffolk line over the River Gipping.

MAIN LINES, STATIONS AND SERVICES

59. Class E4 2-4-0 62783 at Baylham with the 3.55 Bury St Edmunds to Ipswich train on 25 October 1952. The gatekeeper's cottage is also shown on page 127. (Photo by H.N.James.)

60. The station at Bramford looking towards Paper Mill Lane in around 1910. The station was built by the Bury and Ipswich Railway and opened in 1846. It was constructed mainly of timber. On 1 August 1911 buildings on the Bury line were set alight by a spark from a passing locomotive. The west-bound side of the station was totally destroyed along with nearby cottages. A new station was built on the Ipswich side of the bridge. This closed on 2 May 1955 and was demolished in April 1965.

61. Needham Market station in March 1956.

62. Stowmarket station in March 1956.

MAIN LINES, STATIONS AND SERVICES

63. Staff at Stowmarket station in around 1911. The lad sitting on the right is Hugh Ager.

64. The station staff at Stowmarket in around 1910.

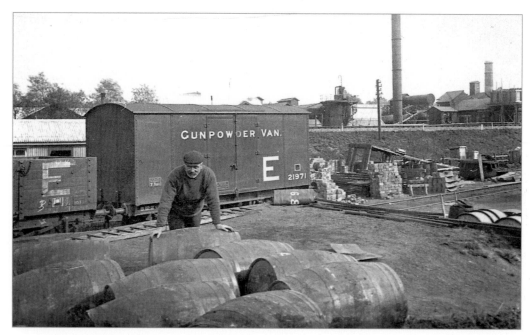

65. A siding at the New Explosives Company, Stowmarket in around 1912. On 11 August 1871 there were two explosions at Prentice's Gun Cotton factory in Stowmarket, which killed twenty-eight people. Some of those killed had arrived at the site after the first explosion.

66. Signalman Alf Spall in the signal box at Stowmarket station. He is rotating the wheel that opens and closes the level crossing gates.

MAIN LINES, STATIONS AND SERVICES

67. Bury St Edmunds station in March 1956 looking west.

68. A British Rail parcel lorry leaving Bury St Edmunds station on a local delivery round in March 1956.

69. A horse used for shunting wagons stands on the line at Finningham station on the Ipswich to Norwich line. The station closed in the 1960s and most of the buildings were demolished although the station master's house remains. Although named Finningham station the site is in the parish of Bacton.

70. A freight train passing through Finningham station. This photograph was taken from the road bridge, now the B1113, shown behind the footbridge in plate 69.

MAIN LINES, STATIONS AND SERVICES

71. On 25 September 1900 a tragic incident at Westerfield station cost two Great Eastern Railway men their lives. The boiler of a locomotive pulling a freight train exploded. 67-year-old driver John Barnard was found scalded and badly injured forty yards from his cab. He died within minutes. Fireman William McDonald could not be found for some time. He was found dead in the third wagon of the train, his clothes in tatters. Also injured by the blast were policeman PC Goodwin, who was trapped in a porter's hut, and a young boy close by.

72. Clearing up at Westerfield station after the explosion of September 1900.

73. B12 61570 crossing the road at Westerfield. This was an East Suffolk line stopping train. The crew on this run were Vic Trenter and Freddie Gibbs.

74. B17 class locomotive 2806 *Audley End* at Westerfield Junction with a northbound train.

MAIN LINES, STATIONS AND SERVICES

75. 61604 *Elvedon* at Westerfield on 3 March 1952 with the 12.40 Sundays Only, Ipswich to Yarmouth South Town train. (Photo by H N James.)

76. Sandringham class 61665 *Leicester City* heading towards Ipswich with the 'up' milk train through Bealings station in the 1950s.

77. B17 class 2808 Gunton at Woodbridge on 14 April 1929 with a 'down' northbound stopping train. The locomotive was just four months old when this photograph was taken.

78. At Woodbridge a B12 locomotive with a train heading towards Ipswich.

MAIN LINES, STATIONS AND SERVICES

79. & 80. Shunting horses at Woodbridge in the 1950s. The horses were used on the Woodbridge tramway as far as Melton until the end of the decade.

SUFFOLK STEAM RAILWAYS

81. Melton station opened in 1859 and became an LNER station in 1923. Like Woodbridge it had horses for working goods traffic. On the left is Charles Wade. This photograph was taken in around 1930.
(Photo by the Titshall Brothers.)

82. Express trains ran from Liverpool Street to Lowestoft and Great Yarmouth. British Railways ran 'The Easterling' along this route. 'The Easterling' was added to the summer timetable in 1950. It was the first titled train to run on the East Suffolk line. It ran in the summer months leaving Liverpool Street at 11.03 am running non-stop to Beccles and then divided with portions for Lowestoft and Yarmouth. Here a B12 61535 is pulling the service through Wickham Market station where the platforms were unusually staggered.

MAIN LINES, STATIONS AND SERVICES

83. Claud Hamilton D16 Class 2590 at Wickham Market junction.

84. B12 61577 heading for Ipswich at Snape junction. (Photo by Dr Ian C Allen.)

85. The railway crossing at Albion Street, Saxmundham in around 1910.

86. 65388 equipped with a snowplough at Saxmundham station in the 1950s.

Ipswich Locoshed

87. Ipswich Locoshed master Richard 'Dick' Hardy. This photograph was taken of him on the footplate of the Mid Suffolk Light Railway's locomotive J15 65447 in the 1950s. The depot off Croft Street Ipswich, on the south side of Stoke Hill was close to the site of the original Ipswich station. The line from Colchester opened 11 June 1846.

SUFFOLK STEAM RAILWAYS

88. Ipswich-based photographers the Titshall Brothers recorded working life in and around Ipswich during the 1920s and early 1930s. Hundreds of their glass plate negatives have survived but not a log of what they show. The photographs on these facing pages are thought to be at the Ipswich Locoshed in the 1920s.

IPSWICH LOCOSHED

89. A footplate crew poses for the camera in the 1920s. (Photo by The Titshall Brothers.)

90. An un-rebuilt Claud Hamilton in the 1920s. (Photo by The Titshall Brothers.)

IPSWICH LOCOSHED

91. Fitters and cleaners at Ipswich Locoshed on a Claud Hamilton class locomotive in the 1920s.
(Photo by The Titshall Brothers.)

92. Engines at the Ipswich Locoshed. On the left is 61647 *Helmingham Hall* built in August 1935 as LNER 2847. On the right is J15 0-6-0 number 65435.

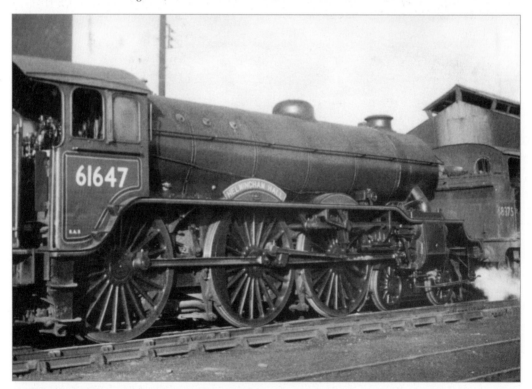

93. B17 61647 *Helmingham Hall* on shed at Ipswich.

IPSWICH LOCOSHED

94. B1 61058 with British Rail staff at Ipswich Locoshed. (Photo by H N James.)

95. 68211 at Ipswich Locoshed with a new diesel shunter 11100 in the 1950s signalling the demise of steam on the dockside trips. (Photo by H N James.)

96. Staff at the Ipswich Locoshed in the 1950s. On the right is timekeeper Harry Aylin.

97. Cleaning up at the Ipswich Locoshed. Richard Hardy's notes say 'Ben Aldous and his Sunday morning cinder gang which kept our yard clean against all odds'. The locomotive was J15 65361.

IPSWICH LOCOSHED

98. Ipswich shed master Richard Hardy (right) with visitors to the Ipswich Locoshed in the 1950s. From the left are K Risdon Prentice, Dr Ian C Allen and Dr Eades. (Photo by H N James.)

99. 62590 at Ipswich Locoshed. With shed master Richard Hardy (right) are Dr Eades (left) and Dr Gonin. (Photo by Dr Ian C Allen.)

SUFFOLK STEAM RAILWAYS

100. B12 4-6-0 61569 with Jock Coleman at the helm passing the Ipswich Locoshed with the 10.15 to Liverpool Street in 1951.

IPSWICH LOCOSHED

101. Class L1 67716 passing the Ipswich Locoshed with the Glasgow to Colchester through train. This was at a time when the Colchester turntable was out of use so tank locomotives, which did not need turning, were used between Ipswich and Colchester

102. A J15 0-6-0 on Ipswich shed with the 'cinders gang' loading ash into wagons.

103. Staff at the Ipswich Locoshed. Details with this photograph, written by shed master Richard Hardy identify the men: 'Albert Southgate charge man, an ex-driver who went colour blind, Les Bloom a real asset, Herbert Rodwell the best list clerk who never became one, Albert Birch a splendid boilermaker's mate, Sam Ford charge man cleaner. We were lucky to have such good men.'

104. The Ipswich Railway cricket team in the 1950s. Back row, left to right: Jack Dye (secretary/ umpire), Ron Bradley, Norman Dye, Dave Ely, Sid Podd, Eddie Gray, Johnny Preston and Ken Rodwell. Front row: Harry Josselyn, Ian Gillespie, Richard Hardy, Bill Brookes and Herbert Rodwell.

105. Eric Birch turning a buffer before burnishing.

106. B1 Class 61056 in the 1950s.

SUFFOLK STEAM RAILWAYS

107. In 1903 James Holden introduced his class C53 0-6-0 tram engines to the Great Eastern Railway. Under LNER they became class J70. They were produced for dock work and on the Wisbech and Upwell Tramway in Cambridgeshire. They were equipped with cow catchers and the wheels, cylinders and motions were enclosed to protect pedestrians and horses. Number 68220 is drawing class B17/4 number 61649 *Sheffield United* out of the shed. (Photo by H N James.)

108. J15 65467 with a dock lines tram engine. (Photo by H N James.)

IPSWICH LOCOSHED

109. Tram locomotive 68224 with shed master Richard Hardy (right) and Jack Percy.

110. A line-up of dock engines. This photograph was probably taken on a Sunday morning. During the week these steam engines were based in a small depot near Stoke Crossing but returned to the main loco shed for maintenance.

SUFFOLK STEAM RAILWAYS

111. LMS Railway-designed 46466 from Cambridge shed being used for the Griffin Wharf trip freight. There is an 'ash' wagon between the brake vans. (Photo by H N James.)

112. Britannia Pacific 70011 *Hotspur* passing the Ipswich Locoshed with an 'up' express for Liverpool Street.

IPSWICH LOCOSHED

113. Fitters and mates, Jack Cage, Eric Birch, Ernie Simpson and Eric Boyle.

114. 68211 on Ipswich shed. This was a conversion of the 0-6-0 to a 2-4-0 with the shortened coupling rod to allow the locomotive to get round the tight curves at Ipswich Dock.

115. Class J39 64826 in clean condition at Ipswich shed. (Photo by H N James.)

116. A Britannia Pacific passing the Locoshed as shed master Richard Hardy looks on. The other
locomotive, 34057 *Biggin Hill* was a West Country Pacific borrowed from the Southern Region.
(Photo by H N James.)

IPSWICH LOCOSHED

117. S Hearsum and B Cage, the largest and smallest employees together at the Locoshed in 1909. This was in a time when boys started work in their early teens.

118. A trio of L1 2-6-4 tank engines, which were predominately used on the Felixstowe branch service. Bill Hart is with the shovel as the photographer's son Robin looks on. (Photo by H N James.)

119. An L1 tank engine about to enter the Stoke tunnel in the 1950s. The train was probably the Colchester to Glasgow service. The Ipswich Locoshed is in the background. (Photo by Aubrey Frost.)

IPSWICH LOCOSHED

120. Shed master Richard Hardy's notes with this photograph say, '5382 was the usual "Wagon and Wheels" shunt. Trams on the tram road for Sunday morning maintenance under Arthur Coleman's guidance.'

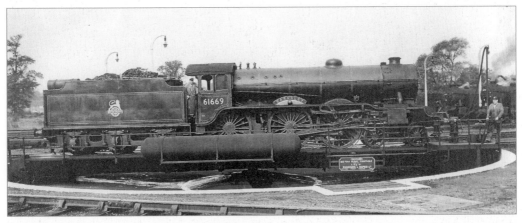

121. B17/4 61669 *Barnsley* on the Ipswich Locoshed's turntable, which was built by the town's engineering company, Ransomes and Rapier. 'Chick' Minns looks on.

IPSWICH LOCOSHED

122.   Locomotive 61645 *The Suffolk Regiment* passing the Locoshed with a train for Liverpool Street.

123. Richard Hardy's notes with this photograph say, 'Three 1500s wait for Sunday afternoon turns to Liverpool Street. A panorama of the old Ipswich depot. Men worked miracles in appalling conditions accepted as normal.'

124. 68555 with a stovepipe chimney. This locomotive was transferred from the Scottish Region to replace scrapped J66 and J67 engines. Unlike the local examples, this engine retained its original low cab roof.

Ipswich Dock and Lower Yard

125. A line from near Ipswich station crossed the River Orwell to serve freight yards and Ipswich Dock with lines to Cliff Quay. Road traffic was stopped as freight crossed the road near Stoke Bridge. This was the Lower Yard from the Princes Street bridge in the 1890s. (Photo by Harry Walters.)

IPSWICH DOCK AND LOWER YARD

126. A panoramic view of the Lower Yard between Commercial Road and the River Orwell in April 1952 as a J69 number 68518 heads towards the Princes Street bridge. (Photo by Aubrey Frost.)

127. This pair of shunting horses was close to Stoke Bridge in around 1930. (Photo by the Titshall Brothers.)

128. A tram locomotive and crew near Commercial Road in around 1930. (Photo by the Titshall Brothers.)

IPSWICH DOCK AND LOWER YARD

129. A Great Eastern Railways T18 tank engine number 292 near the rail bridge over the River Orwell close to Reavell's engineering works in Ranelagh Road in May 1915. The train was loaded with twenty General Service horse-drawn wagons for the Army Service Corps, made by Ransomes Sims and Jefferies at their Orwell Works in the area around Duke Street. Ransomes made 5,000 of these wagons in the First World War period. The Maltings building in the background stands at the junction of Princes Street and Chancery Road.

130. Cattle being unloaded from wagons on a yard near the Princes Street bridge in the 1950s. Tuesday was market day in Ipswich, held on sites off Princes Street. It was common when this photograph was taken in the 1950s to see cattle herded along Princes Street to and from these sidings. This photograph was taken in the same area as the picture above.

IPSWICH DOCK AND LOWER YARD

131. The yard between Commercial Road and the River Orwell from an R and W Paul silo near Stoke Bridge at Ipswich Dock in the mid 1960s. (Photo by Mike Farthing.)

IPSWICH DOCK AND LOWER YARD

132. Wagons near Stoke Bridge at Ipswich Dock in around 1910.

SUFFOLK STEAM RAILWAYS

133. Hard work loading by hand to or from wagons at Ipswich Dock in around 1930. (Photo by the Titshall Brothers.)

134. The Great Eastern Railway Company ran paddle steamers along the River Orwell to Felixstowe, Harwich and Shotley. The three steamers were *Suffolk*, *Norfolk* and *Essex*. Because they could not turn in the narrow river, the three steamers – each with a bow at each end – simply paddled in reverse. This photograph was taken as the *Suffolk* set sail from New Cut West in around 1912.

Mid Suffolk Light Railway

135. 'The Middy'- the Mid Suffolk Light Railway - first carried passengers on 29 September 1908. The line, which ran from Haughley to Laxfield, became known as, 'the railway which ran from nowhere to the middle of a field'. For nearly fifty years the service carried everything including corn, coal, bombs and beet and operated until 1952. This photograph was taken at Laxfield station on either the first or second day of the passenger service.

136. The end of the line by the windmill at Laxfield in the early years of the service.

137. Laxfield station soon after it was opened.

MID SUFFOLK LIGHT RAILWAY

138. Laxfield station towards the end of its life.

139. J15 65388 beside the pond at Laxfield Mill in August 1952. The pond was used to back up the water supply to the tank at Laxfield engine shed. (Photo by Dr Ian C Allen.)

SUFFOLK STEAM RAILWAYS

140. George Rouse operating the crossing gates at Low Road, Mendlesham in around 1949. The fireman was Arthur Bowen.

141. This photograph is thought to have been taken at the same time as the picture above.

MID SUFFOLK LIGHT RAILWAY

142. Mendlesham station in the early years.

143. J15 65447 climbing Haughley Bank. The driver was Ernie Baker with fireman Ronnie Thompson.
(Photo Dr Ian Allen.)

144. A mixed train on the Laxfield to Haughley line with Joe Skinner and Jack Law on the footplate.

SUFFOLK STEAM RAILWAYS

145. A view from the tender of the J15 at Kenton. Ipswich shed master Richard Hardy's notes with this picture say, 'Tim Schofield, variously known as Tiger or Texas, a daredevil character.'

146. J15 65447 on the main line between Stowmarket and Haughley with the afternoon Laxfield train which started at Stowmarket to accommodate Stowmarket Grammar School pupils returning home.
(Photo by Dr Ian C Allen.)

MID SUFFOLK LIGHT RAILWAY

147. J15 65447 at Stradbroke.

148. J15 65467 with the LNER district engineers saloon 690903. There is a water tank under the left wheels.

149. A goods service with Tim Schofield on the footplate. (Photo Dr Ian Allen.)

150. The last train from Haughley to Laxfield arriving at Laxfield 26 July 1952.

MID SUFFOLK LIGHT RAILWAY

151. The last train soon before departure from Laxfield to Haughley 26 July 1952.

152. The last train on the 'Middy' after arrival at Haughley station 26 July 1952.

SUFFOLK STEAM RAILWAYS

153. J15 65388 at Stradbroke picking up empty wagons 6 August 1952.

154. Class J15 65388 at the head of what is believed to be the demolition train on the 'Middy'. This photograph was taken at Laxfield in August 1952. (Photo by Dr Ian C Allen.)

Branch Lines

155. F6 2-4-2 tank 67230 with a mixed train on the Framlingham branch approaching Wickham Market. The Ipswich shed master's notes with this photograph say, 'Jack Turner and Ray Moore giving the impression of going to the end of the earth on the Framlingham branch.' The line opened in 1859, closed to passengers in 1952 and to freight in 1963.

156. Parham station on the Framlingham Branch line.

157. Claud Hamilton D16 62522 at Framlingham station prior to working a through Sunday excursion to Liverpool Street in May 1952. (Photo by Dr Ian C Allen.)

BRANCH LINES

158. A Sunday excursion to Liverpool Street in May 1952 at Hacheston halt. (Photo by Dr Ian C Allen.)

159. Reg Crisp (left) and Eric Browse at Framlingham.

160. J15 65459, believed to be on the Framlingham branch. The white board on top of the buffer shows the train was a special, probably through carriages from Liverpool Street for Framlingham College. Shed master Richard Hardy's notes say, 'A good start up, not permitted, the firebox door shut, in those days smoke was not approved'.

161. & 162. The station at Aldeburgh soon before closure. The station was opened in 1860 and closed in 1966. It was the terminus of an 8½ mile branch line from Saxmundham.

BRANCH LINES

163. Aldeburgh station master Walter Allen with the crew of a locomotive at Aldeburgh station in around 1920.

164. Aldeburgh station master Walter Allen. Mr Allen spent all his working life with the railways. He retired in 1925.

165. Billy Botterill was a porter at Aldeburgh station who took great pride in caring for the station gardens. Billy worked at the station from 1921 until closure in September 1966. He took over care of the gardens in 1922. His work won several awards. Billy was known in Aldeburgh as 'Mr Trains'. This photograph is from around 1960.

166. A J17 0-6-0 on the Aldeburgh branch. Shed master Richard Hardy's notes say, 'Ipswich pinched this old "Knocko" with the vac brake from Norwich or Cambridge, sent it to Aldeburgh and old man Runnacles forgot to put headlights or discs on the front.'

BRANCH LINES

167. 67230 on the Aldeburgh branch near Thorpness with driver Jack Runnacles on the footplate.

168. J17 0-6-0, the Aldeburgh goods at Westerfield with a low tender. There was a tender board to protect crews when running tender first.

SUFFOLK STEAM RAILWAYS

169. Snape branch with a Y14 0-6-0 crossing the River Alde on a wooden trestle bridge. The branch line to Snape was less than two miles long. It opened in 1859 for freight traffic and remained a goods-only line until it closed in March 1960. The line was always worked by steam.

170. A J15 coming off the Snape branch.

BRANCH LINES

171. The Hadleigh branch line from Bentley opened in 1847. The seven-mile track operated a passenger service until 1932. The line closed for freight in 1965. There were stations at Capel St Mary and Raydon. This photograph was taken of J17 locomotive 65578 coming off the branch at Bentley on 4 January 1959. (Photo by Aubrey Frost.)

172. Church crossing at Bentley on the Hadleigh branch line. (Photo by the Titshall Brothers.)

173. E4 62792 fitted with a side windows cab crossing the A12 at Capel St Mary with the 'Suffolk Venturer' rail tour for the Railway Enthusiasts Club on 30 September 1956. Capel St Mary station is in the background. (Photo by H N James.)

174. The same train as above at Hadleigh station.

BRANCH LINES

175. The ticket office at Hadleigh station in September 1949. (Photo by Peter Boulton.)

176. Hadleigh station master Mr S Ellis with driver Ernie Gould at Hadleigh station on 29 September 1949. Ernie was about to drive his last train before retirement. Born in 1884, Ernie started his career on the railway at Parkeston in June 1903. He transferred to Ipswich in 1912. (Photo by Peter Boulton.)

177. The line from Westerfield to Felixstowe opened 1 May 1877. This photograph of the Spring Road, Ipswich viaduct was taken in the 1950s as L1 67708 leads a train from Felixstowe towards Westerfield. The van behind the locomotive was used for prams and bicycles in a period when the non-corridor stock would have been packed with passengers on day trips to Felixstowe.

178. Derby Road station in around 1890. This photograph was taken looking towards Westerfield.
    (Photograph by William Vick.)

BRANCH LINES

179. Class L1 67705 leaving Ipswich heading for Felixstowe past the entrance to the Cranes factory sidings in February 1952. (Photo by H N James.)

180. Orwell station, Nacton with L1 tank 67703 on a special train with guests visiting Fison's at Levington on 7 May 1957. The train came into the platform 'wrong line' to allow ease of boarding for passengers joining the transfer buses to Levington. (Photo by Aubrey Frost.)

181. An L1 tank engine heading towards Felixstowe. This photograph was taken from the road bridge at Levington taking traffic from the village to the main Ipswich to Felixstowe road. (Photo by Aubrey Frost.)

182. A pair of L1 2-6-4 tank engines double heading a train from Felixstowe to Ipswich at Levington.
(Photo by Aubrey Frost.)

BRANCH LINES

183. Trimley station with class L1 67775 (usually the freight engine). This was probably a weekend working from Felixstowe to Ipswich. The train which has passed is heading towards Felixstowe.

184. October 1897. A view from the Mill Lane bridge, Felixstowe as platelayers build the connection between Felixstowe station (to be re-named Beach) and Felixstowe Town. (Photo by Charles Emeny.)

185. When the railway from Westerfield to Felixstowe opened on 1 May 1877 the small tank engine 2-4-0 tank engine *Tomline* hauled the first train. (Photo by Charles Emeny.)

186. May 1877. Three engines were built by the Yorkshire Engine Company of Sheffield for the Felixstowe Dock and Railway Company. This is *Orwell* with one of four wheeled passenger coaches made by the Gloucester Wagon Company. (Photo by Charles Emeny.)

BRANCH LINES

187. Felixstowe station 1883 (later renamed Beach station). The line had been taken over by the Great Eastern Railway Company. The locomotive was GER 231 a Massey Bromley E10 0-4-0, built at Stratford in 1880. Mr Bell the station master is included in the picture. (Photo by Charles Emeny.)

188. The now demolished Beach station, Felixstowe.

SUFFOLK STEAM RAILWAYS

189. 4-4-2 tank engines 6127 and 6125 at Felixstowe Beach carriage sidings before the Second World War. These locomotives were originally built for the Great Central Railway but were transferred to Ipswich for use on the Felixstowe trains in the 1930s.

190. Felixstowe station from the Garrison Lane bridge in 1899 before the second of the island platforms was built between those shown and the goods shed. (Photo by Charles Emeny.)

BRANCH LINES

191. L1 2-6-4 tanks 67703 departing Felixstowe Town. The signals were set for the train to head to Felixstowe Beach.

192. An Edwardian photograph of a carrier at Felixstowe offering to take luggage to local hotels. The backboard has the name G Damant and offers a service from Town, Beach and Pier stations.

SUFFOLK STEAM RAILWAYS

193. A busy Town station, Felixstowe on 2 August 1899.
(Photo by Charles Emeny.)

194. W H Smith's bookstall at Felixstowe Town station in the Edwardian period.

BRANCH LINES

195. The Waveney Valley branch line was from Tivetshall, Norfolk to Beccles connecting the Great Eastern main line at Tivetshall with the East Suffolk line at Beccles. The line was closed to passenger services on 3 January 1953. This was Bungay sation in the 1950s.

196. B12 61577 at Bungay station.

197. The Southwold Railway was a narrow gauge line from Halesworth to Southwold. The line operated from 1879 until 1929. Stations on the line were Wenhaston, Blythburgh and Walberswick. This was the station at Halesworth as one of the line's 0-6-0 tank engines arrived with a mixed train.

198. The tiny corrugated iron station building at Walberswick.

199. An Edwardian view of Southwold station.

Acknowledgements

This book has only been possible with the enthusiastic help of John Day, who along with Graham Hardinge, John Yelverton of the Ipswich Transport Society, Brian Dyes of the Ipswich Transport Museum and David Chappell of the Mid Suffolk Light Railway Museum, have provided me with technical details. Thanks also go to Tom Knights and Norman Dye.

Some of the photographs and information were supplied by Richard Hardy the former shed master at The Ipswich Locoshed, a man whose kind reputation is legendary.

The photographs of Aldbeburgh station were supplied by June Oliver of Leiston, whose grandfather was the station master, and by Derek Johnson of Reydon.

Aubrey Frost was the staff photographer with the Ipswich Engineering company Ransomes Sims and Jefferies from 1956 until retirement in 1991. My thanks to his son Bryan for use of his father's photographs.

Thanks to Mike Farthing who took his camera to the top of a silo at Ipswich Dock to record the yard between Commercial Road and the River Orwell in the mid 1960s.

My thanks also to Nigel Pickover, the editor of the Ipswich *Evening Star,* himself a steam train enthusiast, and Terry Hunt, the editor of the *East Anglian Daily Times,* for the use of photographs taken by the newspapers' photographers. Thanks also for their permission to research information in their archives.

The original negatives taken by H N James are now with the Ipswich Transport Museum. The museum is on www.ipswichtransport museum.co.uk or 01473 715666. Those taken by Dr Ian C Allen are with the Transport Treasury who can be contacted via www.transporttreasury.co.uk.

The Mid Suffolk Light Railway Museum's website is www.mslr.org.uk.

My thanks to all for their help with this book.

David Kindred

A tram engine at Cliff Quay, Ipswich in the late 1920s. (Photo by the Titshall Brothers.)

The crossing gatekeeper's cottage at Baylham. Standing by their home are George and Katherine Carter. Their home was so close to the line it was said that cups and saucers slid across the table when a train roared past! This photograph was taken by the Titshall Brothers in around 1930. See also plate 59.

Other Titles from Old Pond Publishing